THE UNGRATEFUL GARDEN

The Ungrateful Garden

by CAROLYN KIZER

Carnegie Mellon University Press
Pittsburgh 1999

The poems listed are here reproduced with the permission of the following publications, in which they have appeared: *Botteghe Oscure:* "Columns and Caryatids," "The Flower"; *The New Republic:* "What the Bones Know," "Death of a Public Servant"; *The Paris Review:* "On Rising from the Dead"; *The Partisan Review:* "Persephone Pauses"; *Poetry Magazine:* "Complex Autumnal," "The Ungrateful Garden," "The Intruder," "The Great Blue Heron," "A Widow in Wintertime," "A Muse of Water," "Plaint of the Poet in an Ignorant Age," "Love Song," "To a Visiting Poet," "Not Writing Poems About Children"; *Prairie Schooner:* "Epithalamion," "The Damnation," "Hera, Hung from the Sky," "The Old Gods," "The Suburbans," "Birthday Poem for a Childless Man," "Tying One on in Vienna," "The Apostate"; *Trans-Atlantic Review:* "On a Line from Julian," "Linked Verses," "Through a Glass Eye, Lightly"; *New Poems II:* "To My Friend, Behind Walls," "Afterthoughts of Donna Elvira," "What the Bones Know"; *International Literary Annual, Vol. I:* "The Suburbans"; *The Observer:* "The Patient Lovers"; *Inland:* "A Poet's Household," "From an Artist's House."

Library of Congress Catalog Card Number 98-71945
ISBN 0-88748-276-7

The Ungrateful Garden was first published by Indiana University Press, Bloomington, in 1961.

First Carnegie Mellon University Press Edition, April 1999

10 9 8 7 6 5 4 3 2 1

to

THEODORE, DAVID & STANLEY

Contents

for my Mother
September 1880–September 1955

1. THE INTRUDER

Midas watched the golden crust
That formed over his streaming sores,
Hugged his agues, loved his lust,
But damned to hell the out-of-doors

Where blazing motes of sun impaled
The serried roses, metal-bright.
"Those famous flowers," Midas wailed,
"Have scorched my retina with light."

This gift, he'd thought, would gild his joys,
Silt up the waters of his grief;
His lawns a wilderness of noise,
The heavy clang of leaf on leaf.

Within, the golden cup is good
To heft, to sip the yellow mead.
Outside, in summer's rage, the rude
Gold thorn has made his fingers bleed.

"I strolled my halls in golden shift,
As ruddy as a lion's meat.
Then I rushed out to share my gift,
And golden stubble cut my feet."

Dazzled with wounds, he limped away
To climb into his golden bed.
Roses, roses can betray.
"Nature is evil," Midas said.

THE INTRUDER

My mother—preferring the strange to the tame:
Dove-note, bone marrow, deer dung,
Frog's belly distended with finny young,
Leaf-mould wilderness, hare-bell, toadstool,
Odd, small snakes roving through the leaves,
Metallic beetles rambling over stones: all
Wild and natural!—flashed out her instinctive love,
    and quick, she
Picked up the fluttering, bleeding bat the cat laid at her feet,
And held the little horror to the mirror, where
He gazed on himself, and shrieked like an old screen door
    far off.

Depended from her pinched thumb, each wing
Came clattering down like a small black shutter.
Still tranquil, she began, "It's rather sweet. . . ."
The soft mouse body, the hard feral glint
In the caught eyes. Then we saw,
And recoiled: lice, pallid, yellow,
Nested within the wing-pits, cosily sucked and snoozed.
The thing dropped from her hands, and with its thud,
Swiftly, the cat, with a clean careful mouth
Closed on the soiled webs, growling, took them out
    to the back stoop.

But still, dark blood, a sticky puddle on the floor
Remained, of all my mother's tender, wounding passion
For a whole wild, lost, betrayed and secret life
Among its dens and burrows, its clean stones,
Whose denizens can turn upon the world
With spitting tongue, an odor, talon, claw,
To sting or soil benevolence, alien
As our clumsy traps, our random scatter of shot.
She swept to the kitchen. Turning on the tap,
She washed and washed the pity from her hands.

14

THE WORMS

Let Dodo rejoice with the purple worm. . . .

. . . *the worm hath a part in our frame.*
For I rejoice like a worm in the rain. . . .

CHRISTOPHER SMART

This was childhood:
Walking through the worms
After a rain,
Trying not to wound
Anything alive;
Most especially
Not to maim the self
By any kind of death.

Move among the worms,
Pearly and purple,
Curling and opal,
Tickled by the sidewalk,
Heaped over the lines
Of childhood's first map:
Step on a line
Break your mother's spine,
Step on a crack
Break your mother's back.
Take care of mother,
Beware of father,
Protect foot and finger,
My heart and my heel.
Tiptoe on the spaces,
Don't tread on sex!

Life in small forms—
Hop-toads, lobelia,
Moreover, worms,

The recently born—
Whelms us in childhood:
We grow as we move
Close to the ground,
Eyes in our toes.

Crumbling, cool
And many-dimensioned,
The morsels of soil
Cling to a worm
When he comes to rain
Fresh from the ground:
Bruised as a blueberry,
Bare as a rose,
Vulnerable as veins,
Naked as a nose.
The earth-worm smell
Of each commencement,
The sense that the new
Owns all that it is.
When the torrents end,
God gloats at the world.

BY THE RIVERSIDE

*Do not call from memory—all
numbers have changed.*
**From the cover of the
telephone directory**

Once I lived at a Riverside
1-3-7-5, by a real stream, Hangman's Creek,
Named from an old pine, down the hill
On which three Indians died. As a child,
I modeled the Crucifixion on that tree
Because I'd heard two Indians were thieves
Strung up by soldiers from Fort Wright in early days,
But no one remembered who the third one was.

Once, in winter, I saw an old Indian wade,
Breaking the thin ice with his thighs.
His squaw crouched modestly in the water,
But he stood up tall, buck-naked. "Cold!" he said,
Proud of his iron flesh, the color of rust,
And his bold manhood, roused by the shock of ice.
He grinned as he spoke, struck his hard chest a blow
Once, with his fist. . . . So I call, from memory,
That tall old Indian, standing in the water.

And I am not put off by an operator
Saying, "Sor-ree, the lion is busy. . . ."
Then, I would tremble, seeing a real lion
Trammeled in endless, golden coils of wire,
Pawing a switchboard in some mysterious
Central office, where animals ran the world,
As I knew they did. To the brave belonged the power.
Christ was a brave, beneath that gauzy clout.

I whispered to the corners of my room, where lions
Crowded at night, blotting the walls with shadows,
As the wind tore at a gutter beneath the eaves,

17

Moaned with the power of quiet animals
And the old pine, down the hill,
                              where Indians hung:
Telling my prayers, not on a pale-faced Sunday
Nor to a red God, who could walk on water
When winter hardened, and the ice grew stronger.

Now I call up god-head and manhood, both,
As they emerged for a child by the Riverside.
But they are all dead Indians now. They answer
Only to me. The numbers have not changed.

A WIDOW IN WINTERTIME

Last night a baby gargled in the throes
Of a fatal spasm. My children are all grown
Past infant strangles; so, reassured, I knew
Some other baby perished in the snow.
But no. The cat was making love again.

Later, I went down and let her in.
She hung her tail, flagging from her sins.
Though she'd eaten, I forked out another dinner,
Being myself hungry all ways, and thin
From metaphysic famines she knows nothing of,

The feckless beast! Even so, resemblances
Were on my mind: female and feline, though
She preens herself from satisfaction, and does
Not mind lying even in snow. She is
Lofty and bedraggled, without need to choose.

As an ex-animal, I look fondly on
Her excesses and simplicities, and would not return
To them; taking no marks for what I have become,
Merely that my nine lives peal in my ears again
And again, ring in these austerities,

These arbitrary disciplines of mine,
Most of them trivial: like covering
The children on my way to bed, and trying
To live well enough alone, and not to dream
Of grappling in the snow, claws plunged in fur,

Or waken in a caterwaul of dying.

ONE TO NOTHING

The bibulous eagle behind me at the ball game:
"Shucks a'mighty!" coming through the rye
And seven-up, "I didn't mean to kick you, lady.
When you go to the Eagles' convention, you just go!"
Then he needles the batter from Sacramento:
"Too much ego!" he yells. "The old ego curse,
That'll hex him. The old ego never fails.
See?" he says to his phlegmatic friend,
"The bastard fanned!" And "Shucks a'mighty!"
Says again, an American from an English novel,
Named Horace or Homer, a strange colonial bird,
A raw provincial, with his outmoded slang.

"Say!" he cried to his friend, "just now I opened
One eye, saw the catcher, then the batter
In a little circle. And everything went brown.
What happened?" "Nothing!" says his friend.
He leans beside me, proffers the open pint.
My ego spurns him. "Fly away!" I say
To the badge on his breast. Eagle flaps down,
Confides in the man on first: "Just once a year
I have fun—see?—at the Eagles' convention.
Later I meet the other dignitaries
 At the hotel. Forgive me. I'm from a small town,"
He sighs, puts his head in the lap of his friend,

Listens to the portable radio, as the announcer
Makes sense of a blurry ball game
When batters turn brown, curl at the edges,
Fan and fan, like girls in early English novels,
And you can't tell the players, even with a program.
The count is two and one. We hear the crack!
Bat skids across the grass. The runner's on!

But eagle sleeps; he dreams away the ball game.
The dozen wasted hits, the double-plays
Are lost on him, as we lose, by one run.
Having his inning curled in a little circle,
He emerges, sucks his bottle; his badge mislaid

In the last of the ninth. We surge to the exits
While this bird claws among the peanut shells
In search of his ego. Carry him, friend,
To the dignitaries, to the eagle's aerie,
Where his mate will hone her talons on his breast.
As D.H. Lawrence wished, he has cracked the shell
Of his ego, but devoured it like a nut
Washed down with rye. And he finds oblivion
Like the lost hero of a Modern English Novel.
What happens? Nothing. Even the brilliant infield
Turns brown. Lights out. The circle fades below.
Shucks a'mighty. If you're an eagle, you just go.

THE DEATH OF A PUBLIC SERVANT

In Memoriam, Herbert Norman

Envoy Accused of Being Red Kills Self.
Cairo, April 4, 1957.—Canadian Ambassador Herbert Norman committed suicide early today, apparently because of charges in a United States Senate subcommittee that he was a Communist. The Canadian government had denied the charges.
The embassy announced the 48-year-old career diplomat leaped from a high building. It stated he was an "extremely conscientious public servant" and that "recent unpleasant publicity and accusations greatly distressed him."

This is a day when good men die from windows,
Leap from a sill of one of the world's eyes
Into the blind and deaf-and-dumb of time;
Or by ways desperate or ludicrous
Use one of the world's machines for God's,
As George used his gun by the swimming-pool
And was found in the flamingo-colored water,
Or John, drowned in a London crater,

Saw a drowned world there before he plunged:
A baby-carriage frame, a plumber's elbow,
Memorials to his dying as he died;
Now you, in Cairo, and I do not know
How that young, dedicated intellect
Was forced away at last from its long service.
Someone in Parliament says you were "killed by slander."
Wounds to your name were mortal to your mind.

Dead friends, who were the servants of this world!
Once there was a place for gentle heroes.
Now they are madmen who, scuttling down corridors,
Eluding guards, climb lavatory wails
And squeeze through air-vents to their liberation,
Where the sensitive concrete receives them

22

From the world's vast, abstract hate;
So they are smashed to sleep.

Or they, found wandering naked in the woods—
Numbed from the buffets of an autumn storm,
Soaked blissfully in its impersonal furies—
Are wrapped and rescued after a long dark night,
Are bustled into hospitals and baths
While the press explains away their aberrations:
"Needed a rest . . . and took no holidays. . . ."
But even so, they have managed to catch their death.

I mark the fourth of April on this page,
When the sun came up and glittered on the windows
As you fell away from daylight into heaven:
The muck of Cairo, and a world silenced forever.
A poet, to whom no one cruel or imposing listens,
Disdained by senates, whispers to your dust:
Though you escape from words, whom words pursued,
Take these to your shade: of rage, of grief, of love.

COMPLEX AUTUMNAL

I let the smoke out of the windows
And lift the hair from my ears.
A season of birds and reaping,
A level of light appears.

Sun lies in urns on the terrace
Like the cat on the chimney. Near
Fall stirs the curtains, narrow

Ribbons of air nip my fingers.
Warm under foot, the carpet
Reminds my skin I am here.

All things begin together:
Weather and love. The ear
Hears the earth turn; we make an adjustment

To that motion: the dip of the sphere
Into autumn, and rustling music
As the leaves are shaken away. . . .

All things begin together,
Here, as I shake, at the day's
Beginning, with pleasure and fear,

Numb with night's dip and turning
When I weathered love-in-a-sphere,
Like the Siamese cat on the chimney

Mysterious, now, as a vessel,
An ark, or a precious container,
She is smoothing, sunning her fur.

I stand at the window and shiver
As the smoke wreathes out of my hair.
All things begin together:

Weather and love and fear
And the color of leaves, and pleasure.
The waxwings come to the ash trees
That rustle until they are bare.

The birds will wing from the weather
While I stand, still as the harvest,
With the sound of the fall in the air.

WHAT WAS IN A NAME

Thomas Love Peacock! Thomas Love Peacock!
I used to croon, sitting on the pot,
My sympathetic magic, at age three.
These elements in balance captured me:
Love in the middle, on his right hand a saint
And doubter. Gentle à Kempis, Thomas the Rhymer,
Wyatt, Campion, Traherne, came later.

On Love's left hand, the coarse essentials:
Skimp them, and Love, denying, slides away
Into pure Thomas, etiolated sainthood.
Before cock, the satisfying sound of liquid
Which, as it strikes against the enamel basin,
Proclaims a bodily creativity.
Then Love springs eternal; then cock comes

Demonstrating Love. The surname is complete:
Its barbed crest, its thousand eyes, its harsh cries.
Thomas Love Peacock! Thomas Love Peacock!
The person unsung the person ritually sung.
But that was thirty years ago; a child's loving
Of God, the body, flesh of poetry.
I hail the three-in-one, the one-in-three.

THROUGH A GLASS EYE, LIGHTLY

In the laboratory waiting room
containing
one television actor with a teary face
trying a contact lens;
two muscular victims of industrial accidents;
several vain women—I was one of them—
came Deborah, four, to pick up her glass eye.

It was a long day:
Deborah waiting for the blood-vessels
painted
on her iris to dry.
Her mother said that, holding Deborah
when she was born,
"First I inspected her, from toes to navel,
then stopped at her head. . . ."
We wondered why
the inspection hadn't gone the other way.
"Looking into her eye
was like looking into a volcano:

"Her vacant pupil
 went whirling down, down to the foundation
of the world. . . .
When she was three months old they took it out.
She giggled when she went under
the anaesthetic.
Forty-five minutes later she came back
happy! . . .
The gas wore off, she found the hole in her face
(you know, it never bled?),
stayed happy, even when I went to pieces.
She's five, in June.

"Deborah, you get right down
from there, or I'll have to slap!
Laughing, Deborah climbed into the lap
of one vain lady, who
had been discontented with her own beauty.
Now she held on to Deborah, looked her steadily
in the empty eye.

THE SUBURBANS

Forgetting sounds that we no longer hear—
Nightingale, silent for a century:
How touch that bubbling throat, let it touch us
In cardboard-sided suburbs, where the glades
And birds gave way to lawns, fake weathervanes
Topping antennae, or a wrought-iron rooster
Mutely presiding over third class mail?—
We live on ironed land like cemeteries,
Those famous levelers of human contours.

But cemeteries are a green relief;
Used-car and drive-in movie lots alike
Enaisle and regulate the gaudy junk
That runs us, in a "Park" that is no park.
Our greens kept up for doomed Executives;
Though golf embalms its land, as libraries
Preserve an acre for the mind to play
When, laboring at its trash, the trapped eye leaps,
Beholding greensward, or the written word.

What common symbols dominate our work?
"Perpetual care" the library steps with lions
More free than moving kinsmen in the toes;
The seagull is our bird, who eats our loot,
Adores our garbage, but can rise above it—
Clean scavenger, picks clean, gets clean away!—
Past bays and rivers of industrial waste,
Infected oysters, fish-bloat, belly up
In sloughs of sewage, to the open sea.

So much for Nature, carved and animate!
Step in, a minute. . . . But our ankles, brushed
With that swift, intimate electric shock,

Signal the muse: the passing of a cat—
All that remains of tygers, mystery,
Eye-gleam at night, synecdoche for jungle;
We catch her ancient freedom in a cage
Of tidy rhyme. Page the anthologies!
A bridge between our Nature and our Time.

Easily she moves from outer life to inner,
While we, nailed to our domesticity
Like Van Gogh to the wall, wild in his frame,
Double in mirrors, that the sinister self
Who moves along with us may own at least
His own reverses, duck behind his molding
When our phones jerk us on a leash of noise.
Hence mirror poems, Alice, The Looking Glass,
Those dull and partial couplings with ourselves.

Our gold-fish gazes, our transparent nerves!
As we weave above these little colored stones—
Fish-furniture—bob up for dusty food:
"Just heat and serve;" our empty pear-shaped tones!
Home is a picture window, and our globes
Are mirrors too: we see ourselves outside.
Afraid to become our neighbors, we revolt
In verse: "This proves I'm not the average man."
Only the average poet, which is worse.

The drooping 19th-century bard in weeds
On his stone bench, beside a weedy grave,
Might attitudinize, but his tears were free
And easy. He heard authentic birds.
Nobody hid recordings in his woods,
Or draped his waterfalls with neon gauze.
No sign disturbed his orisons, commanding,
"Go to Church this Sunday!" or be damned!
He was comfortably damned when he was born.

But we are saved, from the boring Hell of churches;
We run to graves for picnics or for peace:
Beer cans on headstones, eggshells in the grass,
"Deposit Trash in Baskets." For release
From hells of public and domestic noise,
We sprawl, although we neither pose nor pray,
Compose our stanzas here, like that dead bard,
But writing poems on poems. Gravely gay,
Our limited salvation is the word.

NOT WRITING POEMS ABOUT CHILDREN

Once I gave birth to living metaphors.
Not poems now, Ben Jonson, they became themselves.

In despair of poetry, which had fled away,
From loops and chains of children, these were let grow:

"The little one is you all over. . . . "
They fulfill their impulses, not mine.

They invent their own categories,
Clear and arbitrary. No poem needs them.

They need only what they say:
"When I grow up I'm going to marry a tree."

Children do not make up for lost occasions—
"You'd rather kiss that poem than kiss me."

Creations halts, for denials and embraces,
Assurances that no poem replaces them,

Nor, as you knew, Ben, holds the mirror to them,
Nor consoles the parent-artist when they go.

Poems only deprive us of our loss
(Deliberate sacrifice to a cold stanza)

If Art is more durable to us than children,
Or if we, as artists, are more durable than our love.

Ben, I hope you wrote about your dead son
While you were tranced with pain,

Did not offer up those scenes of the infant Isaac in your mind
For the greater poem; but emerged from that swoon

Clutching a page some stranger might have written;
Like a condolence note, cursorily read and tossed aside.

Perhaps at this extremity, nothing improves or worsens.
Talent irrelevant. No poems in stones.

For once, you do not watch yourself
At a desk, covering foolscap. Denied the shameful relief

Of actors, poets, nubile female creatures,
Who save tears like rain-water, for rinsing hair, and mirrors.

Finally, we are left alone with poems,
Children that we cling to, or relinquish

For their own sakes. The metaphor, like love,
Springs from the very separateness of things.

for my Father

2. COLUMNS AND CARYATIDS

I hang by my heels from the sky.
The sun, exploded at last,
Hammered his wrath to chains
Forged for my lightest bones.
Once I was warmed to my ears,
Kept close; now blind with fire!
What a child, taking heat for delight
So simply! Scorched within,
I still burn as I swing,
A pendulum kicking the night,
An alarum at dawn, I deflect
The passage of birds, ring down
The bannering rain. I indict
This body, its ruses, games,
Its plot to unseat the sun.
I pitted my feminine weight
Against God, his terrible throne.
From the great dome of despair,
I groan, I swing, I swing
In unconstellated air.

I had shared a sovereign cloud:
The lesser, the shadowy twin
To my lord. All woman and weight
Of connubial love that sings
Within the cabinet's close
And embracing intimacy.
I threw it all to the skies
In an instant of power, poise—
Arrogant, flushed with his love,
His condescending praise;
From envy of shine and blaze,
Mad, but beautifully mad,

Hypnotized by the gaze
Of self into self, the dream
That woman was great as man—
As humid, as blown with fame,
So great I seemed to be!
I threw myself to the skies
And the sky has cast me down.
I have lost the war of the air:
Half-strangled in my hair,
I dangle, drowned in fire.

EPITHALAMION

You left me gasping on the shore,
A fabulous fish, all gill
And gilded scales. Such sighs we swore!
As our mirror selves
Slipped back to sea, unsundering, bumped gently there,
The room a bay, and we,
Afloat on lapping, gazes laving,
Glistered in its spume.

And all cerulean
With small, speeding clouds: the ceiling,
Lights beyond eyelids. So you reeled in me,
Reeling.

Our touch was puffed and cloudy now,
As if the most impaled and passionate thought
Was tentative in flesh.
This frail
Smile seemed, in our bodies' wash,
Like a rock-light at sea, glimmering
With all the strength of singleness in space.

Still, you will not turn aside,
Your face fallow, eyes touching.
So I cling to your tendrils of hair,
Our two tides turning
Together: towards and away
With the moon, motionless and sailing.

O my only unleaving lover,
Even in expiring, you reach again.
Thus we may rest, safe in this sealing
As beached, we lie,
Our hulks whitening, sun scaling,

While the small sea-foam dries,
And the sea recedes and the beach accedes,
Our bodies piled like casual timber
Sanded, on this pure, solar lift of hour,
Wreathed in our breathing.

We will exceed ourselves again:
Put out in storms, and pitch our wave on waves.
My soul, you will anticipate my shouting as you rise
Above me to the lunar turn of us,
As skies crack stars upon our symmetries,
Extinguished as they touch this smoky night,
And we exhale again our fume of bliss.

This is my shallow rocking to Orion:
Curling to touch the seaweed at your side.
Wrap my mermaid hair about your wrists
And seal my face upon your resinous eyes.

Foundered on finny wastes, we rest
Till dawn, a gilded layer, lies
Across the pallid sky.
The world's a tinted shell borne up where waves embrace.
Its thin, convolving valve will close and clasp
This love, so blessed:
Our sea-life, swooning as it swims, to reach
Tentacular and cleaving arms that touch
A milky flank, a drowned, reviving face.

PERSEPHONE PAUSES

The lengthened shadow of my hand
Holding a letter from a friend
Tells time: the sun descends again.
So long, so late the light has shone.
Since rising, we have shone with ease:
Perhaps not happiness, but still
A certain comfort from the trees
Whose crests of leaves droop down in tiers,
Their warm trunks veiled by aspen hair,
Their honeyed limbs, the loosened earth
About the roots; while flowers recline
In dusty gardens, rest on weeds,
Those emblems of a passing year.

So be it! As I turn, my train
Is plucked by spikes of summer grass.
No clutch of summer holds me here.
I know, I know. I've gone before.
I glance to my accustomed glass,
The shallow pond, but films of slime
Waver across it, suck the verge
Where blunted marsh frond cuts the air.
But as I stare, the slime divides
Like curtains of old green velour:

I gaze into my gaze once more,
Still veiled in foam. But then, the grim
Tragedian from the other shore
Draws near my shade. Beneath the brim,
In motions formal and austere,
We circle, measure, heel to hem.
He proffers me an iron plate
Of seedy fruit, to match my mouth.

My form encased in some dark stuff
He has bedizened, keeps me hid
Save for that quivering oval, turned
Half-moon, away, away from him
And that excitement of his taste
He suffers, from my flesh withdrawn.

But this unwilling touch of lust
Has moved some gentle part of me
That sleeps in solstice, wakes to dream
Where streams of light and winter join.
He knows me then; I only know
A darkened cheek, a sidelong lower,
My nerves dissolving in the gleam
Of night's theatrical desire,
As always, when antagonists
Are cast into the sensual
Abysses, from a failing will.
This is my dolor, and my dower.

Come then, sweet Hell! I'll name you once
To stir the grasses, rock the pool,
And move the leaves before they fall.
I cast my letter to the breeze
Where paper wings will sprout, and bear
It on to that high messenger
Of sky, who lately dropped it here,
Reminding me, as I decline
That half my life is spent in light.
I cast my spirit to the air,
But cast it. Summertime, goodnight!

THE FLOWER

Two from a pit
Met, as they rose.
For strength, they offered each other their own bright blood
    to drink.
As cupped hands bumped in haste, there flashed some drops
    to soil.
Up sprang a rose.

"I used," he said,
"To sow and reap
In passionate haste, flinging the wild seed
Into the noon-hot trench, or where the unbroken, mooncold
    ground
Lay cauled in sleep.

"But what I reaped
Was not a crop
Of anemones wildly rolling the contours of the hill.
No ocean of marigolds washed the soil in gold.
What struggled up

"Out of the loam
Was a giant mole
With onion eyes, who spoke: 'Be rich and wise, and dig below
Where coarse roots cut a worm to twins.' So I followed him
Into his hole.

"Into the night
I fell away.
Awash from wounds, I heard him scorning: 'Trail your seed!
Fall as it fell, in a shower of nothing. Lie in the dust you made.
And so I lay.

"But later woke
And clambered out,
Not so weak as my wounds, meeting another struggler on the way.
We suffered, and were gentled, to give aid. Out of our surge
     to light
This flower sprouts."

"I dreamed," she said,
"I was with child.
Something fathered a flower in my web of sleep, and then
     a dream
Within a dream told me I bore and buried it all in one grieving
     night.
So I woke, wild

"With loss, dug down
To find my fate.
In burrowing, matter and mould gave way. I fell far upon a
     grave.
Its marking shaft, that must have been the axle of the earth,
Impaled my heart.

"With loamy eyes
That ran, I read
Its epitaph, carved upside-down: 'Here lies
No dream of yours. Only the seed of weeds garlands this
     mourning.'
My wound was dead,

"Deader than I,
The lips a seam
Where no blood sprang. What caused my blood to flow so sweetly
     then,
After we climbed together, hand in brimming hand?"
She paused, to dream.

"Listen!" he said.
"Summon your wits!
What bright flare dies from the world if we pluck this flower?
Or if we pass on to our own ways again . . ."
But milk was streaming from her breast as she bent down
To nourish it.

COLUMNS AND CARYATIDS

I

The Wife:
"I am Lot's pillar, caught in turning,
Bellowing, resistant, burning
With brine. Fine robes laced with sand,
Solid, soon to be hollowed by tongues of kine."

Solid, solitary salt lick, she
Is soon to be shaped by wind, abstracted,
Smoothed to a sex-shape only.
Large and lonely in the plain,
Rain melting her slowly.

So proud shoulder dips with compliance
Never in life. God's alliance with weather
Eroding her to a spar, a general grief-shape,
A cone, then an egg no bigger than a bead.

"I saw Sodom bleed, Gomorrah smoke!
Empty sockets are a joke of that final vision.
Tongueless, I taste my own salt, taste
God's chastisement and derision."

II

The Mother:
"I am God's pillar, caught in raising
My arms like thighs, to brace the wall.
Caught by my own choice,
I willed myself to hold this ceiling.

"He froze me at the moment of decision.
Always I wished to bear weight,
Not in my belly where the seed would light.
That globe is great with stone.
But, over me, the weight of endless function,
My thick trunk set for stress,
My face, showing calmly through guano
No strain, my brain sloped by marble curls
To wedge the architrave.

"The world is a womb.
Neither I nor the foetus tire of our position.
My ear is near God, my temples to his temple.
I lift and I listen. I eat God's peace."

III

The Lover:
"I am your pillar that has fallen.
And now, for centuries of rest
I will regard my breast, my calm hills,
My valley for the stars to travel."

Stripped of all ornament she lies,
Looted alike by conquerors and technicians,
Her curling fingers for an emperor's flower,
Her trinkets in barbarians' museums.
They dust away, but she endures, and smiles,
Accepting ravage as the only tribute
That men can pay to gods, that they would dint them
To raise or decorate themselves, themselves are dinted,
The bruise upon the sense of generations.

So boys will turn from sleep and search the darkness,
Seeking the love their fathers have forgotten.
And they will dream of her who have not known her,
And ache, and ache for that lost limb forever.

THE DAMNATION

Before the adamantine gate, I clear my throat
To summon resonance, collect my epithets and gird my bones,
Prepared to talk my way into Hell.

I beat at the gate till my knuckles turn to cheese.
Rhadamanthus, Mines, Aeacus, I hammer with little words
That thrum in my old, gone pulse, that sting of Tisiphone.

"Let me in! Let me leave the air,
Inhale your sulphurous steam-pits, be massaged with staves.
Best of beasts, I want to burn. Singe my bones!

"Let me lose the shape of self: where is the rack
That rids us of abominable skin?
I want to hear my sockets crack like kindling.

"Can I bend my bones, touch crown to talon in a perfect wheel
Like ancient snake with tail in mouth?
Beset my flesh, its choices. Spend my blood!"

In language stripped from tongue as I wish hot meat from bone,
Verbs active as my standing hair,
I crowd the judges, kneel before the keepers:

"Teach anguish so outrageous that known pain
Will seem as trivial as an ant with one leg gone
Laboring up the mound with a dead fly. Amputate my whine

"So the sound is of wood being sawed in the farther orchard
Mixed with the smell of asphodel, fresh shavings
And apples tumbled on spongy ground.

"Solder lips shut, melt my north and south.
Distribute my precious organs impartially among the larger dogs.
Rake my remains, to smoke away their age,

"Delivered at last from my thought and my things,
My net weight, my engorged heart,
So humbled that my purposes grow grass.

"O sink me as a germ, a seed,
To Tartarus, where worms are grey . . . "
The sentence rains on my upraised fists: "Away!

Here carrion birds swoop down at dark to feast.
Some bulb or bump is left, the prey of love . . . "
I hear a shape that sucks about the gates

Calling its own name, answering itself;
in a chink, displaying its torn grin
As it preens its pulp.

The old men say, as they turn with a clang of clothes,
"A soul without a self? We've selves to burn!"
And after, only a vapour drifting up.

THE OLD GODS

after Heinrich Heine

You full-blooming moon!
Turning the ocean to a wash of gold,
So noon and twilight lap the level beaches;
In the blue pallor of a starless heaven
I see clouds move like statues of the Gods:

Great ghosts of mist and marble. No! They're Gods!
The old Greek gods who ruled the world in joy,
Now abdicated, crowded out,
Parading through the midnight wastes of heaven.

Pantheon of Air! I watch, astounded,
Your giant shapes and mute, mysterious passage.
Ha! There's Kronos, once the King of Heaven,
Who shook Olympus when he shook his hair.
Shock-headed now, he holds and never hurls
The flaccid thunderbolts. Old Zeus,
Old Zeus, you once knew better days,
Enjoying boys, nymphs, hecatombs. . . .
Even the Gods can't live forever.
The young drive out the old, as you drove out
Your Titan relatives, your poor old father.

Here's Hera. How she's fallen
In spite of her anxiety attacks;
Someone else wields the sceptre,
You old ex-queen of Heaven.
Your huge eye, scooped out like a statue's,
The limpness of your calla-lily arms:
How could you strike down or trouble
That God-kissed girl, and her God-given Son?

Pallas Athena passes, aegis and all
Her wisdom could not stave off decay.
You too, Aphrodite, transmuted
In reverse, from real gold to ghostly silver,
Still with your amulets, and lovelier
Than real girls. Beauty, you stir me secretly.
If you gave me, once, that liberal body,
I'd die of shock, like the other heroes you endowed. . . .
Dear Lust, you're now the Queen of the cadavers.

Ares, the War God, turns away,
Casts down his terrible eyes;
And old perpetual-adolescent Phoebus
With a rusty lyre, who once livened up those Olympian dinners,
When Haephistos poured the nectar and waited table;
Poor old cripple! He looks even sadder.
Time, for a long time, has extinguished
The Gods' inextinguishable laughter.

You old Gods, I never cared about you.
I don't feel for the Greeks; I loathe the Romans.
But for you, I sigh. I tremble for you,
Lost Goddesses, dispossessed Gods,
Dead shadows, wandering in the night,
Frail clouds, frayed by the wind.
When I think of those windy deities
Who have beaten you down, and now
Conceal their pleasure at your pain
Under that old-sheep meekness
That is part of their stock-in-trade,
I feel a strange resentment
As terrible as your pride.
I could break down their built-up temples,
Old Gods, and fight on your side:
Fight for your high altars and ambrosial rule,
Altars rebuilt and reeking with sacrificial smoke.
I could even bring myself to kneel,
Call your names, raise my arms, and pray. . . .

After all, when you fought in our little quarrels
You always chose to back the winners.
But I, a man, am more magnanimous:
Now that I've joined the battle of the Gods,
I'll fight on the losing side!

THE APOSTATE

The concluding section of Heine's poem, "Frieden," in which he flagellates himself for becoming a convert to Christianity in order to obtain preferment, is omitted from various editions because, in the words of one critic, "it has all the horrible bad taste of a cold and reasoned sneer." The quotation, near the end of my poem, is from "Frieden."

I, Hypocrite Harry, that Hamburg hand-kisser
Who betrayed himself to Jesus for a few lousy Prussian bucks,
A Judas to his race, baptized Christian Heinrich,
Sold out to the Most High, for a safe sinecure
Which never materialized. H. Heine, Ironist

By profession, ate body and blood of crow for this.
0, 'twas a veritable black, feathered banquet,
A crow-feast, with sell-hate for the first course.
And the entree? His stomach ate itself.
Then from under his coat he produced a dripping bouquet

Of ulcers, to adorn the groaning board.
Then the Humbug Herr Professor, Harry the Hoaxer,
Groaned right back. Jews do. Ask any doctor.
Ask Dr. Heine, expert practitioner and self-surgeon
Who could carve his own carcass in public

Under the chandeliers, on the high-tea tables
Of Her Illustrious Highness; under the hard lights
Of the surgical theatre, he pointed to anatomical charts,
Droned out self-explanations as the scalpel flashed.
In one deft move, Harry uncircumcised himself!

Or he hired a hall, and filled it with the high opera
Of his operation, drew the heavy red plush curtains
As he died on the table. But before that drawn-out aria
Milking his death, he had managed to rush backstage,
Crank up the wind-machine, rattle sheets of tin,

Shower down squibs and colophonium, adjust the Devil's cape
Over his surgical uniform, and trim his halo.
A symphony in red, white and black, he sang his coda
In several voices: wind, heartstrings and brass.
A whole orchestra, he then conducted himself to death.

He draped the red, white and black flag over his corpse
Which rose to take bows, shout "Bravo!" "Bis!" and hiss,
Then fall into the pit of hell, while careful Harry
Stood by the flames with his bucket of sand,
Passing out pogroms—er—programs for his Farewell Tour.

So hate Harry. So do him a favor!
Who first wrote *Gelobt sei Jesu Christ*
To conclude a paean to peace. Utopian Harry!
Who dreamed the machines would stop, the streets be clean,
The samite-clad palm-wavers meet with chaste brow-kisses.

I dreamed they saw a huge Christ in the sky,
Holding the sun in His breast: a great Sun-heart
Slowly bleeding on the pure crowd below,
Thrice blessed. . . . Irrepressibly pagan Harry,
That's the Jesus of Mexico, of a Jew enchanted by pantheons.

Then I, Heinrich, wrote *Gelobt sei Jesu Christ*
Again, for the world-as-it-is: "where holy water
Does double duty, washing souls and thinning tea,
And you kiss the crosses, lap-dog paws and snooty faces
Of the most high, pious and respectable:" Harry, Society's toy,

Prepared to praise Christ, if Her Illustrious Highness
Bestowed a raise in pay. But Honest Harry never did.
Heinrich, fish of Christ, and flesh of Zion,
Harry the cock, crows again at the dawn of Greece.
So Kronos, Jupiter, Venus, Elohim, Christ the Jew,

Bless the poet, Heinrich, as he blesses you.

TYING ONE ON IN VIENNA

Variations on a theme of H.H.

I have been, faithfully, to the 39 birthplaces of Beethoven;
To 39 birthplaces of Beethoven have I been.
Reborn, every time, to the wrath of landladies
Who objected to the noise,
He had to move on.
Damn and bless your peripetia, Beethoven.
I am above your Meer und Stürme, I have won my haven
On high, below, in a cozy rathskeller in Vienna.

I tip the whole world down my throat,
Thirsty as Beethoven.
If I were home, I'd float on an ice cube like a polar bear
In my terrible fur, bulky as Beethoven,
Dipping my toes in an ocean of whiskey.
But here is a whole world in a golden brew:
Viennese cathedrals, where Mongol troops, I'm told,
Took pot-shots at gargoyles, to destroy their evil-eyes—
Never mind: gargoyles will rise again, gargle golden wine,
Giggle in rathskellers; Luther broke things too,
Or his followers did. Give me a golden Pope
Who wallows in artifacts, tithes a thousand villages
For one gold goblet: O I see all the Leos of all the Romes
In this glass: Agamemnon's cup, the brilliant vessels
Of Vaphio, with ruminating bulls, bulls grazing,
And bulls chased round and round the bowl by crazy Schliemann.
Turks and Hellenes, Mongols, Shakespearean scholars—Hegel!
Continuity is all!
Changing the petticoat guard at the palace of Paul
And Frederika; orange groves, All Souls' Day, 4th of July parades;

Vienna, Spokane, Los Angeles County—even Hamburg. . . .
And over all others, the face of my lover,
A man with the brain of an angel!

Beloved, thou art fair,
With hair the color of Solomon's beard
And a big head, like Beethoven.
David the Goliath, patron saint of Florence,
Has a navel like a pigeon's swimming-pool;
You are the David of the Galleria dell'Accademia
Whose navel is a little golden bowl
In which I plunge my nose—Oh, what a heavenly odor!
Landlord, hold me up by the hair
Before I drown!

Der brave Mann! We sit here together
Drinking like brother and sister,
We hug each other like sister and brother
And he speaks to me of the power of love.
I drink to the health of my ex-husband
And other enemies, known and unknown.
I FORGIVE ALL LOUSY POETS
AS THEY SHALL FORGIVE ME.
I weep in an excess of feeling!

Then I cry to him, "Landlord, where are the twelve apostles,
The holy hogsheads, hidden in the back room
Where they preach to the United Nations?
Lead me to them, in their plain wooden jackets,
Looking like Mennonite farmers. Their souls are more radiant
Than the Court of St. James's, than the Fabergé eggs
In the Hermitage Museum. . . .
Purple and Gold! My old High School colors!"
O those grand autumn days, when we crushed Immaculate
    Conception,
And the Society of Jesus provided cheerleaders,
Though both teams flopped down on the field to pray

Just before game-time. And I debated the girls from the convent
On, "Resolved: We should have government ownership of rail-
    roads"
And God was on my side, the affirmative.
Though I spoke with the tongue of gargoyle and angel,
God and I lost, because the girls of St. Mary's
Kept their skirts over their knees and their hands folded,
While I waved my wild hair, and bit my nails
In an excess of feeling. . . .

Hooray! I'm being fanned by palm trees!
And the scent of orange groves in the sweet San Fernando Valley
North of Los Angeles, where I spent my childhood;
What an odor of myrrh is rising from a thousand navels!
Reel on, you rivers of the world!
Even the rathskeller door, with its broken hinges
Since the Russian troops hammered it down, looking for girls,
Even the old door, wounded with bayonet marks,
Dances and reels, and my soul staggers for joy,
And we are all healed together, noble Viennese landlord!

He will steer me upstairs to the daylight,
Du braver Ratskellermeister,
And we'll see, though the gargoyles are broken,
There are angels on the roofs of the cathedral,
On all the roofs—see those angels sitting there like pigeons?
Angels of Heine and Rilke, all drunk. Singing,
Hallelujah and Yippee! If there were a sun overhead
It would be red like the nose of a drunkard,
Behind all that Viennese rain, as drunk as Beethoven
Every time he was born. The soul of the world is a nose,
A nose in a navel. The red sun sets in the navel of heaven.
God save a disorderly world, and the wild United Nations!
The twelve holy hogsheads will roll forth on their keg legs
And save us all: poets, Mongolians, landlords & ladies, mad
    musicians.
And we'll reel on together, sing in a widening circle,
Hooray for purple and gold, for liquor and angels!

for my Children

3. A MUSE OF WATER

A MUSE OF WATER

We who must act as handmaidens
To our own goddess, turn too fast,
Trip on our hems, to glimpse the muse
Gliding below her lake or sea,
Are left, long-staring after her,
Narcissists by necessity;

Or water-carriers of our young
Till waters burst, and white streams flow
Artesian, from the lifted breast:
Cup-bearers then to tiny gods,
Imperious table-pounders, who
Are final arbiters of thirst.

Fasten the blouse, and mount the steps
From kitchen taps to Royal Barge,
Assume the trident, don the crown,
Command the Water Music now
That men bestow on Virgin Queens;
Or, goddessing above the waist,

Appear as swan on Thames or Charles
Where iridescent foam conceals
The paddle-stroke beneath the glide:
Immortal feathers preened in poems!
Not our true, intimate nature, stained
By labor, and the casual tide.

Masters of civilization, you
Who moved to river bank from cave,
Putting up tents, and deities,
Though every rivulet wander through
The final, unpolluted glades
To cinder-bank and culvert-lip,

And all the pretty chatterers
Still round the pebbles as they pass
Lightly over their watercourse,
And even the calm rivers flow,
We have, while springs and skies renew,
Dry wells, dead seas, and lingering drouth.

Water itself is not enough.
Harness her turbulence to work
For man: fill his reflecting pools.
Drained for his cofferdams, or stored
In reservoirs for his personal use:
Turn switches! Let the fountains play!

And yet these buccaneers still kneel
Trembling at the water's verge:
"Cool River-Goddess, sweet ravine,
Spirit of pool and shade, inspire!"
So he needs poultice for his flesh.
So he needs water for his fire.

We rose in mists and died in clouds
Or sank below the trammeled soil
To silent conduits underground,
Joining the blind-fish, and the mole.
A gleam of silver in the shale:
Lost murmur! Subterranean moan!

So flows in dark caves, dries away,
What would have brimmed from bank to bank,
Kissing the fields you turned to stone,
Under the boughs your axes broke.
And you blame streams for thinning out,
Plundered by man s insatiate want?

Rejoice when a faint music rises
Out of a brackish clump of weeds,
Out of the marsh at ocean-side,
Out of the oil-stained river's gleam,
By the long causeways and grey piers
Your civilizing lusts have made.

Discover the deserted beach
Where ghosts of curlews safely wade:
Here the warm shallows lave your feet
Like tawny hair of magdalens.
Here, if you care, and lie full-length,
Is water deep enough to drown.

AFTERTHOUGHTS OF
DONNA ELVIRA

You, after all, were good.
Now it is late, you are kind.
Never too late, to my mind.
The mind catches up with the blood.

You, it is good to know,
Now we are not in thrall,
To me were as kind as you would,
Being the same to all.

Those that are true to one
Love not themselves, love none.
Loving the one and many,
You cannot be true to any.

True to your human kind,
You seemed to me too cruel.
Now I am not a fool,
Now that I fear no scorn,

Now that I see, I see
What you have known within:
Whenever we love, we win,
Or else we have never been born.

PLAINT OF THE POET IN
AN IGNORANT AGE

I would I had a flower-boy!
I'd sit in the mid of an untamed wood
Away from tame suburbs beyond the trees.
With my botany-boy to fetch and find,
I'd sit in a rocker by a pot of cold coffee
Noodling in a notebook on my knee,
Calling, "Flower-boy, name me that flower!
Read me the tag on that tree!"
But here I sit by an unlit fire
Swizzling three martinis
While a thousand metaphors doze outdoors,
And the no-bird sings in the no-name tree.

I would I had a bug-boy
With a bug-book and a butterfly-net,
To bring me Nature in a basket of leaves:
A bug on a leaf by the goldfish bowl;
I'd sit in a rocker, a pocketful of pine-nuts
And a nutcracker knocking my knee,
Cracking nuts, jokes, and crying to my bug-boy,
"Read me the caterpillar on the leaf,
Count the number of nibbled veins
By a tree's light, in fire!"
While I, in my rocker, rolled and called,
A caterpillar crawled on the long-named leaf.

If I had a boy of Latin and Greek
In love with eleven-syllable leaves,
Hanging names like haloes on herb and shrub!
A footnote lad, a lexicon boy

Who would run in a wreath around my rocker
To kneel at my chair, at my knee
Saying, "Here is your notebook, here is your pen!—
I have found you a marvellous tree!"
But all I have is a poetry-boy,
A bottle-cap king: he cries,
Thudding from the garden, "What do you call
The no-bird that sings in the no-name tree?"

BIRTHDAY POEM FOR A
CHILDLESS MAN

This is the birthday of your death;
Some odd and forty years ago
The hard light caught you, catching breath
To broach your first, protesting cry.
At birth we leave and enter death,
The bloody pit, the water's tomb;
The knife that cleaves us into love
From love and mother, cuts us back,
Removes the spleen, the gut, the gland,
Till we return to woman's land.

Each form encompassed by the hand
That brought it forth, to soothe the eye
That weeps before the burning light,
To smooth the battered skull, an ear
Turned in against a world of bright
Sensation; in a lapping tide
Of dark, the buried pulses trip.
Caught like a bird, the naked wrist
Flutters in the surgeon's grip.
What woman makes, such men will carve
And shape to fullness, though it starve.

My starveling love, your birthday comes
To mind us of that only cry:
Its bare astonishment at fate,
The cold, the air, the spectrum's shock,
The severance from a throbbing stalk,
The burst of outrage and of pain
That love, who made you, thrust you out.
Because you could not cry again,
I wept, too late! was borne away
In silence, from your clamorous look.

If life unman you at the first,
And all its creatures carry breath
Of carrion, that stinking ghost,
How can you help but turn aside
When love and troubles come to plead?
You suffer, will not suffer me
To bear, to parturate and bleed.
You will cut down your life instead.
So to be male, of woman born,
You make a birthday of my death.

THE GREAT BLUE HERON

M. A. K., September, 1880–September, 1955

As I wandered on the beach
I saw the heron standing
Sunk in the tattered wings
He wore as a hunchback's coat.
Shadow without a shadow,
Hung on invisible wires
From the top of a canvas day,
What scissors cut him out?
Superimposed on a poster
Of summer by the strand
Of a long-decayed resort,
Poised in the dusty light
Some fifteen summers ago;
I wondered, an empty child,
"Heron, whose ghost are you?"

I stood on the beach alone,
In the sudden chill of the burned.
My thought raced up the path.
Pursuing it, I ran
To my mother in the house
And led her to the scene.
The spectral bird was gone.
But her quick eye saw him drifting
Over the highest pines
On vast, unmoving wings.
Could they be those ashen things,
So grounded, unwieldy, ragged,
A pair of broken arms
That were not made for flight?
In the middle of my loss
I realized she knew:
My mother knew what he was.

O great blue heron, now
That the summer house has burned
So many rockets ago,
So many smokes and fires
And beach-lights and water-glow
Reflecting pin-wheel and flare:
The old logs hauled away,
The pines and driftwood cleared
From that bare strip of shore
Where dozens of children play;
Now there is only you
Heavy upon my eye.
Why have you followed me here,
Heavy and far away?
You have stood there patiently
For fifteen summers and snows,
Denser than my repose,
Bleaker than any dream,
Waiting upon the day
When, like grey smoke, a vapor
Floating into the sky,
A handful of paper ashes,
My mother would drift away.

THREE LOVE POEMS

1

Lovemusic

Come, freighted heart, within this port,
Bring all your bee-collected sweet,
The savor of a liberal night,
The crown of columbine, still-wet,
The muse of days. Bring your delight
To fill the palate and the plate,
To rinse the lips. Unburden, set
Your lilies on my chair of state.

Come, laden love, to this, my cave.
For here we soon may hide and move,
In havens play the courting dove,
And pace the newly-altared nave:
This vested place, this heart alive.
With fruit and wine and coupled play,
Each self will give itself away.

Come candidly, consort with me,
And spill our pleasure for a day.
Let love delay, unhurriedly,
This passing taste—I prophesy:
Remembered cinnamon and lime
Will fructify a bleaker time.

The Patient Lovers

Love is an illness still to be,
Still away, another chill.
We shall measure mercury

Of the rising, falling will,
Of the large and resting heart,
Of the body, not quite still,

Still enough to keep the chart
From reflecting what we feel:
We shall be well, and well apart.

Though my body still will start
When from my milky side you steal,
And breathing is a casual art,

And illness we no longer play
Until we fill the healer's part.
We will be well, and well away

Until our pulse and pallor tell
That we are ill, of being well.

3

Love Song

O to fall easily, easily, easily in Love
As nursling birds tumble from the nest
(not—pray—into the dog's jaws).
True lovers of women tend to love
Not grossly, but in gross lots
"Without deduction for tare, tret or waste"
(Webster says), love every look,
Think each new taste the best.

O to fall in Love, easily, easily
As a mild child falls to, at the breast
(not as an iron-jawed child clamps on),
To inhale all sweet ambience, breezily
Exhale flowered breath
While rapturously curls the pillowed fist,
Toes clenched in comfort,
Each new taste the best.

O Love, easily, easily, easily to fall
As fledgling bird or child is lost
(within a plot, not acres away)
Only to turn around, and find the haven
That has not moved at all.
Learn lose-and-find without much cost,
Terror smoothed in feathered, ruffled bosom,
And easily, Love, easily to rest.

A POET'S HOUSEHOLD

Three for T.R., in the Tanka form

1

The stout poet tiptoes
On the lawn. Surprisingly limber
In his thick sweater
Like a middle-aged burglar.
Is the young robin injured?

2

She bends to feed the geese
Revealing the neck's white curve
Below her coiled hair.
Her husband seems not to watch,
But she shimmers in his poem.

3

A hush is on the house,
The only noise, a fern
Rustling in a vase.
On the porch, the fierce poet
Is chanting words to himself.

FROM AN ARTIST'S HOUSE

for Morris Graves

1

A bundle of twigs
On the roof. We study pictures:
Nests of hern and crane.
The artist who built this house
Arranged the faggots there.

2

Is the inlaid box
With a gilt hasp concealing
A letter, a jewel?
Within, a bunch of feathers,
The small bones of a bird.

3

The great gold kakemono
With marvelous tapes and tassels,
Handles of pale bone,
Is a blaze on the wall. Someone
Pinned an oak-leaf to the silk.

4

Full of withered oranges,
The old, lopsided compote
Reposes on the sill.
Poor crockery, immortal
On twenty sheets of paper.

LINKED VERSES

for Donald Keene

Read a thousand books!
Consult your dreams! Drink spirits.
Then write your poem.

The poet, tossing pebbles,
Muses on rings within rings.

When the rains descend,
Life, that was buried forever,
Sends up a cool green flame.

What is as new as a toad!
The unborn calls to the born.

Pricked on the furze-bush,
You reached for the kindling axe
And forgot the blossom.

So rough, they catch on the silk,
How shall my hands keep busy?

Gold chrysanthemums
Have the faint, acrid odor
Of Mortality.

Pain, ugliness, old age:
At least they make no demands.

The frost was late this year:
Crystal nips the petals,
As my lover grows impatient.

The blind worm says to his brother,
"Who will need us when we die?"

ON A LINE FROM JULIAN

I have a number and my name is dumb.
Living for death, this paradox I take:
Such a barbarian have I become.

Because historians are growing numb,
They will not say we love what we forsake,
To be a number when a name is dumb.

Our leaders urge us further to succumb.
Our privy hearts in unison must ache,
Says a barbarian. Have I become

A vessel that is empty of aplomb
To ornament the century's mistake,
And be a number when my name is dumb?

Subsisting on a drop of blood, a crumb,
When wine is gone, and bread too hard to break,
A small barbarian have I become.

I can be private in delirium,
Indifferent to the noises that I make.
I have a number, and my name is dumb.
Such a barbarian have I become!

WHAT THE BONES KNOW

Remembering the past
And gloating at it now,
I know the frozen brow
And shaking sides of lust
Will dog me at my death
To catch my ghostly breath.

I think that Yeats was right,
That lust and love are one.
The body of this night
May beggar me to death,
But we are not undone
Who love with all our breath.

I know that Proust was wrong,
His wheeze: love, to survive,
Needs jealousy, and death
And lust, to make it strong
Or goose it back alive.
Proust took away my breath.

The later Yeats was right
To think of sex and death
And nothing else. Why wait
Till we are turning old?
My thoughts are hot and cold.
I do not waste my breath.

TO A VISITING POET IN A COLLEGE DORMITORY

Here tame boys fly down the long light of halls
In this late nightmare of your fourth decade:
Medley of shoe-thuds, towel-slaps and horseplay,
Murmurous radios, counterpoint of squalling
Bed-springs and shower-pipes across your ceiling.

Nocturnal soundings turn you back always
To a broken fountain, faces damp as leaves
Stuck to the fountain's lip in autumn, draining
From an era swamped in war's impersonal seas.
Do you sleep empty and long, or cannonading

Through these nautical chambers, having gathered all
Your strength into one battered bowling ball,
Asleep, ramp up and down these corridors of boys
Barely knocking at doors, but bursting into
Identical rooms, like icicles ablaze?

Now, as I hope you sleep, I turn the pages
Of your committed life—rather the notations
Of sensation coaxed and cheated into poems:
Loves are interred three deep, or rise like drowned
Ruined choristers, to flaunt your praises.

Fisher of bodies, when the lure is failing,
Still you proffer the old nibble of boy-bait,
Though nothing comes now, arias or kingdoms;
You may not deny death, nor contrive it soon.
Only escape, your orphanhood outrun,

Run from the glisten of those refracting egos
Where you could love and loathe yourself on sight,
To the worst priesthood, or test-tube remedy
For fratricidal passion. Run from the children!
To father men and poems in your mind.

ON RISING FROM THE DEAD

Lift up in lilac-emerald breath the grail
Of earth again—
                    Thy face
From charred and riven stakes. O
Dionysus. . . .

HART CRANE

Saturday noon: the morning of the mind
Moves through a mist to breakfast: damp from sleep,
Rustic and rude, the partial self comes down
To face a frozen summer, self-imposed;
Then, as the numb shades lift, becomes aware
Of its other half, buried overhead,
A corpse in twisted sheets, a foggy portrait
Smudged in the bathroom mirror—elegies
Sung on the nerves of a pillow-muffled phone.

Nobody's home at home, the house announces.
And the head nods, nobody's home in here.
The bird of dawning silent all day long,
Nobody's home to nobody abroad:
As cars curve past the house, taking themselves
For airings, while the drivers doze within;
Anonymous dogs chivvy the ghosts of cats
Safely locked in the basement. Apples nod
Their hard green heads, lost in a blur of leaves.

Last night, in the hot house, the self sang
Its oneness, in reflection of a love.
Now the cold fragments rise, remembering;
As feudal lieges move for a missing King
Shattered on plains of sleep, they summon armies:
The midget fingers, elbows, eyes and toes,
To patch again the china egg. And horses,
Masculine cavalry of the will, prance, pull
The egg, in cobweb harness, up the hill.

80

So the self trots upstairs, and reunites
With its lost half, by towelling off the mirror.
Reluctantly, the self confronts the self
Ripped, untimely, from its naked bed,
The winding sheets tossed down the laundry chute.
The room's aroma: whiskey and ripe fruit
Stale with fulfillment, while picked flowers curl
Their lips, like suicides in brackish water,
Soiled Ophelias, whom no breath can fulfill.

Still, air the rooms! though fruit and flowers cry,
"Leave light, leave air to buds! Beyond bloom,
Who cares?" Get thee to a compost heap.
Renew, the self prays to decay. Renew!
And buckles on its shell to meet the day,
Puts off the fantasy these rooms recall,
Of apple-chasing goddesses, a King
Raining his arrows in the laden trees
That weaponless, drop their pears in sticky grass;

Goes out-of-doors, to its own daylight domain
Where, pomegranate red, a mole on the lawn
Shrieks to the person from its several parts:
A Dionysus, dismembered by the cats
In a community of sharing: "Here! You keep
The head. I love a bloody leg!
They must have sung in harmony, dragging limbs
About the yard; then left the god unburied,
The raw material of a ritual.

Last night this purring priesthood was caressed
Before the cellar lock-up: smelling gamey,
The smoke from incense-fires in their fur;
Dark-jawed from feasting, they had toyed with Kings'
Tossed organs, skinless as the summer moon!

So self and mole shared midnight, and the twain
Lay sundered on their fields. What rose again
To mend its wounds by fading Saturday?
A solar King, a subterranean mole?

Or both? Did severed parts personify
The prince of Darkness and the prince of Light?
Kicking, meanwhile, this body from the lawn,
Interring bits below the apple tree
Where the foot turns loose earth around the roots
And tamps it down. But nostrils of the cats
May raise the dead. So be it: What's a grave
But plunder, to a gardener? Or a priest
Rooting up bones of martyrs for display.

The other body takes itself to bed,
Buries itself in sheets as thin as soil,
Dreams of the elevation of the Host:
Mole in a silver chalice; kneels to sup
The blood of the dying, resurrected soul.
But there is leaping in the chancel aisle;
Stale altar flowers toss their heads, and burst
In an orgy of bloom: Communion Sunday,
With Dionysus, singing from the Cross!"